DAVID

Retold by Anne de Graaf
Illustrated by José Pérez Montero

B&H
BROADMAN
&HOLMAN
PUBLISHERS

DAVID

Published in 1999 by Broadman & Holman Publishers,
Nashville, Tennessee

Text copyright © 1998 Anne de Graaf
Illustration copyright © 1998 José Pérez Montero
Design by Ben Alex
Conceived, designed and produced by Scandinavia Publishing House

Printed in Hong Kong
ISBN 0-8054-1899-7

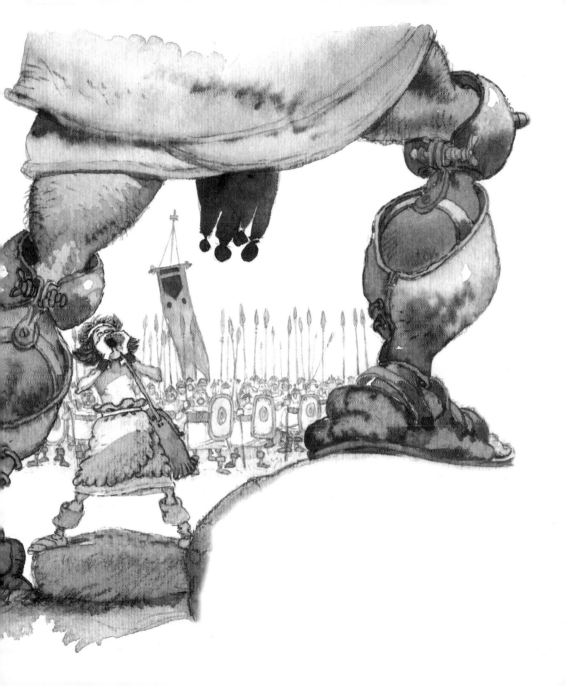

When God looked at the heart of a shepherd boy named David, he saw that David loved God very much.

Can you look at your heart? Can you feel it? Oh no! Don't get tickled!

David liked to play his harp
and sing songs for God.

9

David was also very good at slinging stones. He could hit whatever he aimed at. He could even kill bears that hunted his sheep.

He could EVEN kill lions
with his sling!

13

A wise man named Samuel came to David's family to find God's choice for king. Not this brother, not this one, not this one, not this one, not this one, not this one, not this one!

15

"Are these seven boys all your sons?"
Samuel asked.
"No," David's father answered. "I have one
more. The youngest."
God chose David because God had plans for
him. Not now, but someday David would
become king.

Sometimes being the youngest isn't so bad.

Who was the enemy everyone was
so scared of? A big, huge giant!
And the giant's name was
GOLIATH!

What is a bully?

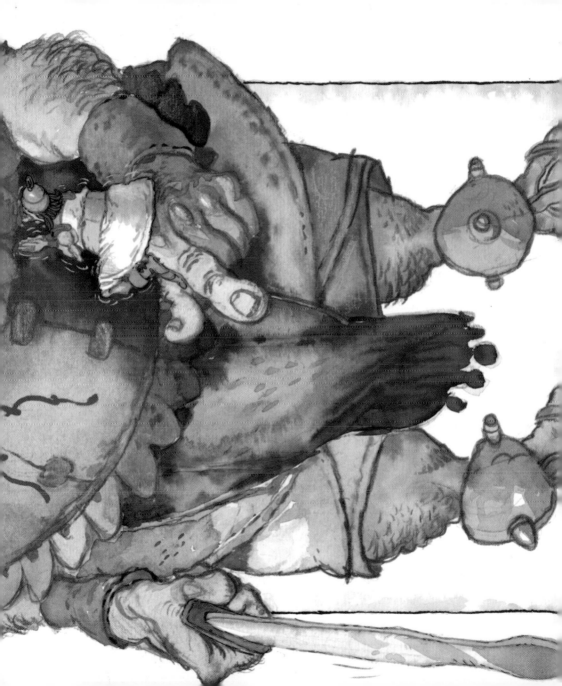

One day the army of Israel had to fight a terrible enemy. All the soldiers were very, very, very scared. David was too small to be in the army like his brothers.

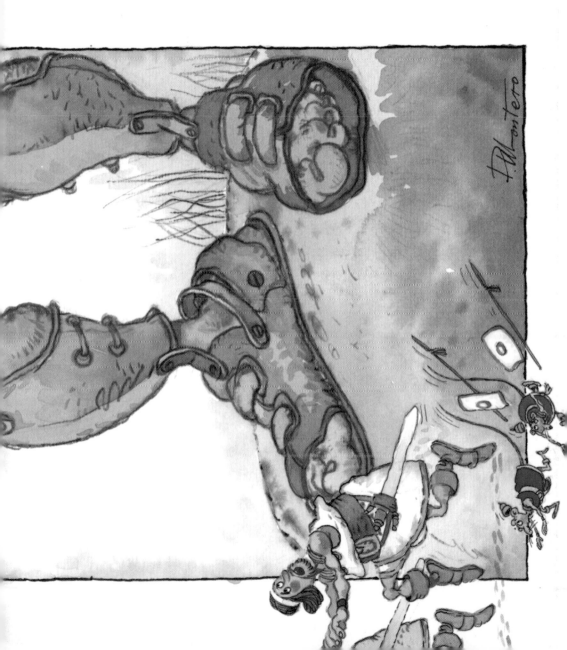

No one in the army dared to fight the giant. But David begged King Saul, "Let me fight Goliath!"
Saul said, "You're just a boy."
David said, "I'm good with a sling."

David knew
God was on
his side.

27

The giant Goliath was making fun of God and God's people. "You're nothing, and so is your God!" This was a terrible thing to say. David said, "Oh yeah? You're not too big for me!"

Has anyone ever made fun of you because you're the smallest or youngest?

David took aim at the giant and
sent a stone whistling through the
air with his sling. The stone flew
and flew until. . . . "PING!" It hit
Goliath in the head. David had
killed the giant.

*It's not always the big and
strong who win. Sometimes
it's the small and brave.*

31

After David killed
Goliath, everyone said,
"Three cheers for
young David! Hip, hip
hooray! Young David is
brave and handsome."

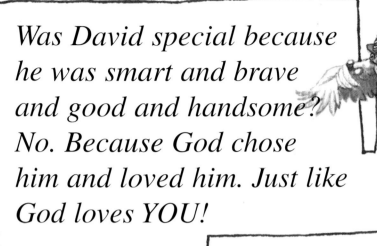

Was David special because he was smart and brave and good and handsome? No. Because God chose him and loved him. Just like God loves YOU!

33

Some time later, God's plans
for David finally happened.
David the shepherd, David the
brave, David who loved God
so much he sang for him, this
David became king of Israel!

God promised David that his family would last forever. This happens through Jesus. God loved David's heart because David wanted more than anything to be close to God.

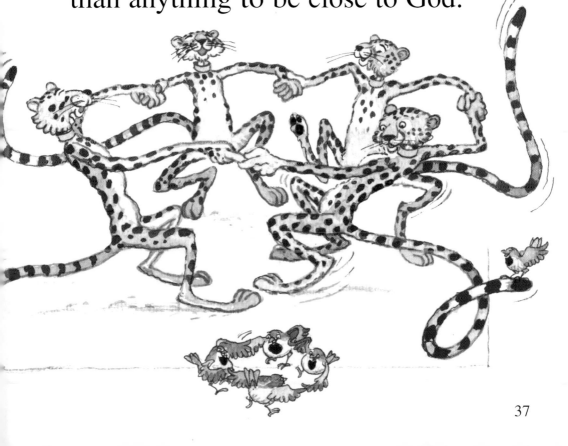

A NOTE TO THE big PEOPLE:

The *Little Children's Bible Books* may be your child's first introduction to the Bible, God's Word. This story of *David* makes the first letter of Samuel, chapters 16 and 17, spring to life. This is a DO book. Point things out, ask your child to find, seek, say and discover.

Before you read these stories, pray that your child's little heart will be touched by the love of God. These stories are about planting seeds, having vision, learning right from wrong, and choosing to believe. *David* is one of the first steps on the way. The Bible story is told in straight type.

A little something fun is said in italics by the narrating animal to make the story come alive. In this DO book, wave, wink, hop, roar, or do any of the other things the stories suggest so this can become a fun time of growing closer.

Pray together after you read this. There's no better way for big people to learn from little people.